Of Elderberry,
Fire, & Fables

Of Elderberry, Fire, & Fables

Bridgette Valentine

Querencia Press – Chicago IL

QUERENCIA PRESS

© Copyright 2024
Bridgette Valentine

All Rights Reserved

No reproduction, copy or transmission of this publication may be made without written permission.
No paragraph of this publication may be reproduced, copied or transmitted save with the written permission of the author.

Any person who commits any unauthorized act in relation to this publication may be liable to criminal prosecution and civil claims for damages.

ISBN 978 1 959118 95 4

www.querenciapress.com

First Published in 2024

Querencia Press, LLC
Chicago IL

Printed & Bound in the United States of America

*For those who feel both too rotten and too sweet
and know that the two are sisters.*

CONTENTS

Toothy 11
Crowing 12
Not a Thought in My Mind 13
Elderberry Sister 14
Copper 15
Tuesdays Belong to Us 16
A Hunger 17
A Box in the Basement 18
When 19
Devilish 20
Saturn Return 21
Pretty Late 22
Horse Girl 23
How It Looks 24
Olive 25
Crop Circle 26
Alice 27
Telephone Poles 28
Northern 29
Bunks 30
Apple Cider 31
For Eve 32
Cannibal 33
Wiser 34
Eons 35
Taurus 36

Daughter	37
Despite	38
Ice Queen	39
Wraith	40
Yawn	41
Snake	42
Splinters	43
In Spite	44
Beast	45
Evergreen	46
When the Sun Goes Out	47
Toad	48
Rotten	49
A Flicker	50
You First	51
Spent	52
Antler Velvet	53
Acknowledgments	55

Toothy

    Everything bathed in light equates to healing. The life I've cultivated doesn't need to be touched by grief.

    The best parts of life are sugary sweet. Dipped in caramel and promises. Stop bringing my inner child into the conversation and reminding me I'm rotten.

    Cavities become missing molars and fuzzy, forgotten strawberries I forgot to indulge in. Now I'm spitting up blood and small parts of me in the form of jagged teeth.

CROWING

A little bit of girlhood, a little bit of cherry wine.

Crows begin to rest in the corners of our eyes. Our laughs leave residue like stardust in the creases of our cheeks. Silver strikes strands of hair like lightning in a rain storm, leaving us forever changed. Age leaves its mark.

But we are fables. We are legends. We are in our girlhood, forevermore in our little corner of the cosmos.

Not a Thought in My Mind

I like to feed into my heart. Burrow deep inside of it. Travel through vessels like empty door frames into lifetimes beyond myself.

In another universe, I'm not so angry.

I'm not somehow lackluster and too intense in the same breath. I don't second-guess myself. I don't wonder if my words are wrapped in subconscious malice instead of kindness. I don't run cold and spite isn't the only way to get me heated.

In another universe, I am soft.

So soft that my skin is made of pink rosebud petals and my eyes are droplets of morning dew. Each night, they fall from their sockets between my dandelion lashes, washing away the day and any loathing they have seen. Opening at dawn as a fresh set drops from a spiderweb overhead.

I am always ready to see the world through new eyes.

In another universe, my words are always wrapped in lavender and a gentleness that spreads like kudzu. In another universe, I've never crossed paths with someone like me.

It never occurs to me.

Elderberry Sister

 Buttercup, knobby knees, shallow breath and holding back, bite my tongue, try to fit in.

 Daffodils, giving lip, scratched cd's, and blushing cheeks. Full of rage, just like you taught me.

 Dandelion, first crush, tangled hair and mangled words, sour candy. All meeting the same end.

 Youth is such a wild thing. Poison oak, poison ivy, elderberries.

COPPER

Open your mouth and let me slide my tongue so deep inside that you can tell me my words taste tart as unripened raspberry.

Loosen up your wisdom tooth, wrap it in copper, wear it dangling atop my collar bones.

I want every set of eyes to know all your thoughts are mine.

Tuesdays Belong to Us

A little cabin. A space for me and you. I'll pick us cherries, you draw the curtains so the sun shines through.

Maybe we'll get married. Ordained by the moon. Breathe my vows into your lips. Keep your tongue tied 'til noon.

And if there's a chance of a forever someday, it looks a lot like your freckles and feels a lot like a Tuesday.

Twirl me in our kitchen. Waltzing on creaking floors. Lift me up like always. Pull me in, leave your stress at the door.

Maybe we'll live forever. The sun will go out and so will the moon. But I can stand the dark if it holds me to you.

And if there's a chance of a forever someday, it looks a lot like your freckles and feels a lot like a Tuesday.

A Hunger

I want the real thing. That bottomless pit kind of devotion. That peach pit sweetness. That even the thought of its absence feels like a tongue to a dagger. That longing, that yearning, that hunger for that something more.

A Box in the Basement

Where did it come from anyhow? I don't know where to set it down.

A vase in fumbling, sweaty palms. The pet names you gave me. The stories about your family.

So much hurt between us over the course of moons and birthdays and silent dinners. So much affection between us over the course of sunsets and new year's eves and polaroids.

You see me, I see you.

Crowded rooms where you're just out of reach. Deserted rooms where neither of us will take the first step. What feels like a lifetime between us. I can look at anything but you.

I've seen you be devious. I think it rubbed off on me. I think it was always there.

You told me about the unsavory parts. The way grief lives with you and the way your chest caves in.

So many times I tensed up in the face of vulnerability. So many times I laughed in its grace. So many times I regretted it with the sound still caught in my throat.

I don't know how to fix it. It's a part of me now. You are a part of me.

So where does it all go?

When

If I don't write about it, only write to you—is it real then?

If I stifle my moans it's like they're not really happening.

If I bite down on my tongue when it wants to be inside of your mouth—is it real then?

If I only say your name between breaths it's like you're not really happening to me.

Devilish

    I'm growing devil horns out of my skull and they feel like heaven. Sharpen them against the bones of fabled men. Their tavern song voices stay trapped inside of me and whistle through skeletal tree branches. Groans distorted into moans on my perked ears. Each year I've taken leaves and a pine tree's ringlet awakens around each horn. It's almost matrimonial.

Saturn Return

Your name won't live in the heath of my heart once the chill of autumn dusts off the cobwebs of us.

I moved through the walls of our home like a woman in white. A revenant with youth in her still. In the realm of existence but with an otherworldly grief. Phrases spoken that feel like prophetic, contrasting parallels now.

"I feel like a ghost in my own home."

A ghost doesn't receive love letters or soliloquies, she's only written about in obituaries. The flowers were always wilting in our secret garden because I was rotting underneath.

When I mourned the pink rose bush, you said, "Don't worry, it'll come back even if it looks dead right now."

I made the most of the poppies and weeds, knowing even wild things need a place to rest. Now our garden is coming up shades of pink again just like you said, but I'm still six feet deep.

Funeral flowers for a banshee.

Pretty Late

For a moment, I was tangible. I was flesh and bone and blood tangled up with you. My heart stained us red with every word that spit from my mouth. The fact that I too was afraid of the dark petrified you.

There we were, no nightlight, nowhere to run.

I heard your heart creak as you pulled away from me. I heard monsters shuffle under the bed and then I realized that they were us too.

Horse Girl

Some days I wish I were easier to swallow. I'm a tough pill built for a horse to choke on. When they bury her behind the stables, they mark the grave with a rock and a handmade wooden cross.

I am not always easily digestible, but it's important to remind myself that I am more delicate than I've been led to believe. I am not all bramble and the smoldering of dead leaves. I am here only for a moment and I will leave softer than I was welcomed into it.

How It Looks

Mourning. Morning. Two sugars?

Olive

    Lately I've been burning olive branches. Tying knots in cherry stems, solo slow dances. Brought a hurt pigeon in, lied and called it dove while I bandaged it.

    Do you think my body wants to get rid of me the way I want to get rid of it? Call me a dove, wrap me in bandages.

    My words have scorch marks, ashen and falling apart. My words are a flaming house these days.

Lately I've been burning family trees.
I wear my father's eyes so they won't say a thing.

    My hair grows in brown as a burr. Little pinecone girl, don't you know it's time?

    Do you think the land wants to get rid of me the way I want to get rid of it? Gasoline and bristles, nothing else makes sense.

    My words have scorch marks, ashen and falling apart. My words are a flaming house these days.

CROP CIRCLE

    Crop circle year, slowly coming of age. Thoughts you didn't know you had, urges that just popped up. When the whole family gathers round to gander, you stay quiet as a stalk, quiet as dinner at the table.

    Oil lamp year. Dimly lit love burns the farmhouse down. Douse the open flames 'til you're reminded that you look the same. Burning, yearning, and a house-sized crop circle pops up.

    When the whole town gathers round to gander, you stay quiet as a mother, quiet as dust on the mantle.

Alice

    White rabbits living in canvas, above where I rest my head and dream of sheep embroidered with numbers and arbitrary recollections of the day.

    Perfume that smells like strawberry shortcake and the summer solstice. Ruffled socks I pair with my sneakers and boots, so I may always walk with an air of whimsy. Tattoos of ivy vines and cherubs and cicada wings to transform myself into a fairytale illustration.

Telephone Poles

    We are velvety pillow talk between telephone wires.
Whisperings that taste like whiskey and peaches.
Take that taste and swish it from your mouth to mine.
One day I'm going to down the whole bottle.
I want to taste like you.

Northern

No more pine trees. They've been traded in for cobblestone streets and sanctuary. A singular mulberry bush in the backyard and enough nettle to hide from neighbors.

I miss the evergreens but I don't miss the dread that accompanies me when I travel back in time. The peach pit that lives in me now isn't weightless, but it's light enough. Every day I shed a few more feathers.

Tonight I drive home to fresh sheets and warm, ambient light. I harmonize with the sound of my twenties to a playlist I named August. I smile with every word. Just grateful to experience these human emotions.

There are no deer when I signal at the bodega—not even the stars can be seen here, just outside the city—but all of the lights that guide me home are green.

Bunks

    Sharing a room with my sisters. Our bedside table lamp is older than us. You can hear the electricity inside of it buzzing with life.

    I almost forgot that there was a time when you could see the static tangibly build in front of the wooden tv that sat on the floor.

    We are somewhere in the midst of it.

Apple Cider

Cinder my bones like October cider, so eager to be inside. Crumble me down to bramble and brush me aside like silk secrets.

Ashes to ashes and dust to dust because I can't bear the thought of leaving behind any semblance of myself in the place that made me burrow.

For Eve

    Something full of shame and hemlock troubles me to ask Eve for her forgiveness. Age has skewed my sight. I see her in blinding, starry-eyed stained glass, at last.

    A snake slithering restless with compassion. A man's heart bursting with so much devotion that he never once misses his other rib. Half a lifetime at her side. All those who wander into her darkness will meet banishment and decay. All the misconceptions in the flesh. All the reasons I cannot blame her.

    God will see me kiss her hands, her thighs. Please her for praise and repentance. I will listen to her list her wicked ways—in moans and between sighs. I will spell my sins out with my tongue.

    God will have to crawl to me for forgiveness.

Cannibal

Ravel me in your gossamer. Make a meal out of my neck. To be tangled in your web, a lucid dream.

WISER

      We are olive branches, set afire. We are cherry trees, set ablaze. We are here to witness it all.

      We are splintered crucifixes, we are bushy-tailed, running through tree lines. We are here as omens.

      We are wax seals, we are curse words written in calligraphy underneath. We are laughing at the grass stains on our Sunday best.

      We are grave dirt, we are hand-picked wildflower bouquets resting on the mounds of fresh earth. We are wise when we know to be.

Eons

Against the deadly nightshade and eons of story-telling, I have been offered comfort by my finiteness under this same moon across lives and ancestry. I have felt so small and I have felt so infinite.

I wonder in how many lifetimes I've made time for the stars. That I've looked to the heavens for fellowship. Our bones hold traces of stardust. The very structures that hold us up are molded in folklore and creation.

I think I am homesick.

Taurus

 Little bull-headed babe, rearing its head in the depths of the woods. Do your horns hurt as they break the skin? Have you broken them in yet?

 Little ram, you little battering ram. Do your words still rake against the coals of your throat as you search for diamonds? Do you destroy the mine shafts when you're left only with soot-covered hooves?

 Little horned calf, always split in half between a rock and a hard place. Does your crown of rage burn atop your head? Do you feel it radiating through your bones?

 I hope you tire of the heat of despair and find a time to rest against the moss. A pillow for a weary traveler. A well-deserved rest. I hope you find this moment before the dusk finds you.

 So many before you have wandered restless past the witching hour, the devil's hour, and well into the dawn of a new day. I do not want to see your touch-starved carcass on the horizon with them along the mountain ridges.

 Little bull, lay down your horns. Lay down your armor. Rest.

Daughter

    Wake up in the middle of the night, moonlight shining through the blinds. Drink my moon water. What a gift to be the son,

    but I am the moon's daughter.

Despite

I have built churches on the parts of myself where he burned my flesh so bright that I thought I would never sleep again. I have planted roses in every pore of my body just to pluck them and put them on the graves of all the girls I used to be. I have tasted how sweet my future children's names are as they roll off my tongue in sleep.

Ice Queen

    I must admit, I wonder if you'll ask to see me on your deathbed. If when you start seeing that bright light glimmer through the blinds in your hospital bed, it will thaw you.

    I wonder if I'll still be here, frozen in time with a cold fire-ache. I wonder if I'll be given peace if I let my spiteful dreams come true.

Wraith

    I want to be the girl that haunts your skin. A ghost town every time a thought of me creeps in.

    You taste divine and then me too. A vineyard graveyard and my perfume. She moans at night, oh she wails, for you in the twilight.

    Pine for me. Pine to call me pet names. Like dear or darling. Fall in love with ghostly singing—the voice that, before, only a mother could love—lullaby of a wraith.

Yawn

I've been living in the fog, convinced that I am trapped in purgatory. Cursed by the eyes I had to say goodbye to.

I feel nothing and everything. Words and feelings drip out in agonizingly slow motion. Stretched out like a yawn.

Snake

    There is nothing more thrilling or as devastating as shedding your skin. Growing into and out of yourself. Fangs in flesh and viper venom in each dawn.

Splinters

    I mourned you and I'll burn you too. Pouring gasoline on everything. On the threshold and the family Bible and the stolen library books. Pour it in my wounds right after the salt and call it an heirloom recipe.

    A few years ago I would've sopped up the mess 'til my knees were bruised from kissing the floor, my tongue now ripe with splinters. But the only thing older is me and I'd sooner light the match against my crooked teeth.

In Spite

Wisteria crawling up myself. Always beside myself, in spite of myself. Winding myself up, knowing well enough that the only way I know to wind down is through the gutters.

Beast

    You—Heart of soft spring. Easter lily laughter. Fairy dust eye flutters.

    Me—Devouring your heart of spring as if I will never have another April again. Bloody, quiet thing now resting in my soft underbelly.

Evergreen

    Summer solstice, evergreens. Freckled nose and heart covered in burrs. Checking for ticks and poison oak and other undesirables. Growing pains so sharp you feel it in your bones. The earth builds you up just to take you down with it. Growing pains so sharp you whimper through your bedtime story. The same way you did when you saw your friend's heart was a different shade of grief than your own. You used to have their landline memorized.

    Scraped knees and green bottle-neck caffeine. It rains every year on your birthday. Late August, the last day of Leo season, heart of a hurricane. History documentaries with your dad. It was the only time his words were calm. You noticed your first patch of gray this past winter. You remember him fighting time the same way he fought everything else.

    You have your moment, you let it be. Only trees are evergreen. Count them again on the equinox. Thank time for allowing the company.

When the Sun Goes Out

My heart has changed. It is glowing so faintly,
it lends its existence as a nightlight. Always for the sake of
others. It wants to burn up like the end of the universe
instead of this burning down like a candle stick.

Toad

    Leave this world, you devout little toad. So comfortable in your creekbed. In your sludge and waste. Spawning, undisturbed, your shining tadpole eggs.

    Did you resent them for growing legs? When they surpassed you and evolved past the same waters young men washed blood off their hands by baptisms?

The very same that made virgins of the girls for the boys' pleasure once again.

    Did softer words get stuck in your throat? Were you in your own way? Did you croak? Will you please?

Rotten

"Does it get better?" *Tell me it gets better.*

"Never got that sorry." *Don't think I ever will.*

"Our house was loud." *Our house was empty.*

"I thought about it. Telling people you died."

Your name is Absent. Your name is A Ghost. Sharing genes makes me feel so rotten. Right down to the core. A poison apple.

I thought about it. "But why should I?"

A FLICKER

Every year is a flicker, a beat of the heart.

I'm unsure if my heart was ever a child's or if I was born with the weight of the world and brittle bones inside of me. Ever since I was a girl, I whimpered that my bones hurt. Some nights I still do.

Life felt so long until late. Girlhood was a millennium and my early twenties was a decade. Only now, at the peak of my happiness, is every year a blink. Nearly thirty and I see fifty peering from between the slants of the blinds.

There's something endearing there. There's wisdom I haven't yet uncovered. There are parts of my heart to be unveiled through a lifetime that will feel like an hour.

Every year is a flicker, a beat of the heart.

You First

If I rest my head beside you to slumber and wake up the next morning in another lifetime, I'll go find you first.

Before coffee, before the sun has fully risen, before your touch has gone cold on my skin. In every universe, I will seek out your heart. In every reality, I believe I'll hear the call of our existence.

I will always try to find you.

Spent

 When I pull up the bundles of thistle and deadnettle, bits of earth underneath my nails come too.

 I fill the woven basket further with sharp pine needles and rotting mushroom spores and it's soon packed to the brim.

 It doesn't feel like mine to carry anymore.

Antler Velvet

Make a tonic out of all the days you thought you couldn't endure. Mixed with antler velvet and blackberry blood.

As you grind them with your mortar and later again with your teeth, they ask only that you remember the lives within them and now yourself.

The buck and his fawn mother. Birdsong as the morning dew sets. The bramble that protected them both.

ACKNOWLEDGMENTS

Of Elderberry, Fire, & Fables has been such a long, transformative journey to write. At the tail-end of my twenties, this book feels like growing into myself. Coming to terms with parts of myself I struggled to claim and saying goodbye to a chapter in my life. It's coming of age in its own rite. It's been thrilling, devastating, and I find myself vocalizing more gratitude than ever before.

Now onto sharing some of that.

I'd first like to thank Querencia Press and its founder, Emily Perkovich, for giving this book a home. Emily encouraged me to make *Of Elderberry* whole and find its real identity. I like to think it's an older sister. This wouldn't be the same art without them in my corner.

To those I love and uplift me at every turn, thank you a million times over. I'm still learning to own my accomplishments. This book is such a labor of love at its core.

And last but not least, thank you, dear reader. My first poetry book was largely centered around grief with little specks of light in between. This book feels like the other side of that grief as I become more grounded in myself and reality. I hope that if something resonates, you're coming out of the other side as unscathed as possible. Or at the very least, I hope you're able to find yourself and a semblance of peace.

Until next time.